LEARNING CENTERS for First Reconciliation, First Eucharist, and the Whole Community

Doris Murphy

TWENTY THIRD 23rd
PUBLICATIONS

Twenty-Third Publications
A Division of Bayard
One Montauk Avenue, Suite 200
New London, CT 06320
(860) 437-3012 or (800) 321-0411
www.23rdpublications.com

ISBN 978-1-58595-564-0

The Scripture passages contained herein are from the *New Revised Standard Version of the Bible*, copyright ©1989, by the Division of Christian Education of the National Council of Churches in the U.S.A. All rights reserved.

Library of Congress Catalog Card Number: 2005935875
Printed in the U.S.A.

Table of Contents

Introduction 1

Learning Centers for First Reconciliation

1. Building Self-Esteem 4
2. Families Forgive 6
3. Making Peace with God and Others 8
4. Making Choices 10
5. Conversion and Reconciliation 12
6. Being Sorry 14
7. The Ten Commandments 16
8. How Many Times Must I Forgive? 18
9. The Holy Spirit Guides Me 20
10. Examine Your Conscience 22
11. Steps for the Sacrament of Reconciliation 24
12. Preparing for the Sacrament 28

Learning Centers for First Eucharist

1. God Loves Us 32
2. The Last Supper 34
3. The Mass 36
4. Tour of the Church 40
5. Objects Used for Mass 44
6. The Apostles Creed 48
7. Words about the Eucharist 50
8. The Loaves and Fishes 53
9. Jesus, Our Shepherd 56
10. Prayer 58
11. We Are Many Parts 62
12. I Am the Vine 64
13. Baptism 66
14. The Church 68
15. Preparing for First Eucharist 70

Learning Centers for the Whole Community

Celebrating Forgiveness	74
Examination of Conscience	76
A Sign of God's Mercy	78
Forgiving Others	79
Prayer and Ritual	80
The Church	81
Breaking of the Bread	82
The Mass	83

Appendix

Letters to Parents	85
Evaluation Form	87
Group Gathering Prayers for First Reconciliation	88
First Reconciliation Prayers for Individual Families	89
Group Gathering Prayers for First Eucharist	90
First Eucharist Prayers for Individual Families	91

Introduction

Learning centers, at first commonly called learning stations, are an example of a paradigm shift in education. This new model or method for learning seems to have sprung up simultaneously in many places at once. At first, learning centers were used for math, science, and geography, as schools searched for interactive ways for children to better grasp what they were expected to know. Educators also wanted to provide for the different learning styles and abilities of children and allow them to work at their own pace. Thus creative teachers started developing learning centers, stations, or stops where learners could complete a specific activity—with tools and directions provided—on their own and following their own timetable.

Directors of faith formation around the country began to examine the possibilities of using this model with learners and parents as they explored new ways to "hand on the faith." They discovered that because this model can be used with almost any doctrinal content, it is a practical way to involve parents more fully in preparing their children for the sacraments of reconciliation and Eucharist.

The learning centers in this book are meant to supplement whatever textbooks children are using. They offer families and children the opportunity to work together informally as they share faith and prepare for the sacraments. Learning centers help families do this in a non-intimidating, educational, and enjoyable way. For the whole community, they offer a way to spend meaningful time with parish children while joining in the process of learning about and living the faith. As with any parish endeavor, this "whole community" aspect is very important.

Learning centers for sacrament preparation have many additional benefits. They give children the opportunity for interactive and creative learning about reconciliation and Eucharist, in addition to what is covered in their textbooks. They give families the opportunity to do hands-on tasks with their children and thus discover new ways to share their faith. Both parents and children learn more about the sacraments in this kind of informal setting. Learning centers also offer the opportunity for more flexible scheduling of sacrament preparation classes. They give directors of faith formation the opportunity to observe children and parents working together, and thus determine which centers offer the greatest learning opportunities.

A few practical points:

- If possible, before the families begin their visits to the learning centers, review briefly with them the sheet of directions: the goal, the Church teaching, what they will learn, etc.

- Make copies of the suggested readings from the *Catechism of the Catholic Church* and post them at the appropriate centers so those who wish can read them.

1

- Make certain that each center has all the supplies needed, and enough of each supply.
- For each center, put a marker on the page where the families can find the Bible passage for that center.

The learning centers in this book have been successfully used in several parishes with very positive feedback from both children and families. We hope you will also find them valuable and well worth the time it takes to organize and set them up.

These learning center activities can be scheduled in two ways. All participants can come at the same time, for example from 4:00 to 6:00 PM on two different evenings. Or families can come during a span of time at their own convenience, for example on a Saturday afternoon between 1:00 and 5:00 PM. (Encourage families to allow at least two to three hours to thoughtfully visit all the centers and complete the activities.) In the Appendix you will find Gathering Prayers that you can use with both options.

Special thanks to Carol Mercord, Religious Education Director at St. Joseph Parish in Prescott, Wisconsin, for her support and helpful advice as she used these learning centers, and to Barbara Havel for her endless patience in helping me prepare this manuscript.

Learning Centers for First Reconciliation

Building Self-Esteem

Goal

To understand that self-esteem and self-worth are gifts from God. These gifts help us love God, self, and others.

Church Teaching

Catechism of the Catholic Church, paragraphs 307, 1700–1876

What You Will Learn

To recognize that everyone has dignity and worth

To recognize that God's forgiveness is for everyone

Supplies for this Center

Bible

Game board, dice, and markers (buttons, pennies, markers from other games, etc.)

Directions for the Activity

• Together, read Genesis 1:26–31. What does this passage teach us about our dignity and worth?

• To use the board game, We Are God's Work of Art! determine who begins.

• Throw the dice and move the marker as indicated by the numbers on the dice.

• Follow the directions on the space on which you land.

We Are God's Work of Art!

(Ephesians 2:10)

Start Here

What is something special that makes you happy?

I am happy!

Ways I can share talent I have with others.

What is your talent?

Tell the person to your right something special about him/her.

What is SPECIAL about you?

Thank God for someone who makes me feel good.

I feel good!

Ways I can let each family member know how much I appreciate him or her.

My family is special!

Something I do that makes me feel good about myself.

I am unique!

Thank God for something I like about myself.

I'm glad to be me!

I am a good friend when...

Friends are special.

The Bible tells me so... Look up and share
*Isaiah 43:1 & 4
*1 Corinthians 3:16-17
*Luke 1:49
*Matthew 10:29-31

We are made in God's image.

Send messages (words) that make others feel good about themselves.

I love you!

Families Forgive

Goal

To reinforce that it is within the family and/or church community that we learn forgiveness.

Church Teaching

Catechism of the Catholic Church, paragraph 1657

What You Will Learn

To "make up" with family members whom you have hurt

To experience forgiveness within your family

Supplies for this Center

Bible

Four to six pencils, glue

Worksheet: Ways to Make Up, one for each family

Small 2 x 2 pieces of various colors of tissue paper, approximately six pieces per person

Directions for the Activity

- Together read Luke 19:1–10. Share what this passage means to you. What made Zacchaeus happy?

- Discuss with one another the need to "make up" with those we have hurt. Give an example of how forgiveness can be experienced anywhere, but especially within your family.

- Together fill out the worksheet and complete the suggested activity. Glue several pieces of tissue paper together to make a flower for your sheet as a sign of forgiveness.

Ways to Make Up

Zacchaeus was forgiven. He made up for any wrong he had done by paying back what he had taken (Luke 19:1–10). We, too, can make up when we have done something wrong.

Complete the following sentences

When I quarrel with a family member, I make up by _____

When I disobey a rule, I make up by _____

When I am unkind to a sister or brother, I make up by _____

When I hurt someone in my family, I make up by_____

Here are some ways I can make up

Admit I was wrong.

Ask for forgiveness.

Try to do better.

Shake hands or hug.

Paste your tissue flower here

Making Peace with God and Others

Goal

To learn that the sacrament of reconciliation calls us to make peace with others, to be reconciled with them. It also calls us to be reconciled with God.

Church Teaching

Catechism of the Catholic Church, paragraphs 1657, 2840

What You Will Learn

To talk about the words "apologizing," "loving," and "forgiving"
To name people who need or want your forgiveness
To think about ways to thank, ask forgiveness, and apologize to others

Supplies for this Center

One coupon booklet for each child
Four to six pencils
Stickers to decorate the coupons (optional)

Directions for the Activity

• Read Matthew 5:23–24. Discuss ways to make peace with others in your home, your school, or the world.

• Give your child one of the coupons. Ask him or her to quietly think about others they should forgive or to whom they should apologize. Discuss this with them.

• On the coupon have the child write his or her name and the name of the one to receive it. Suggest that he or she decorate it. (Encourage him or her to actually give it to the person when appropriate.)

My Reconciliation Coupon Booklet

✂ -

To: _____

I am sorry for: _____

Please forgive me! This coupon is good for one hug!

From: _____

♡

- -

To: _____

I am sorry because: _____

I will try my best to do better. Please forgive me!

From: _____

☺

- -

To: _____

Thank you for loving me all the time! I am trying to be
the best I can be!

From: _____

♡

- -

To: _____

I apologize for my words or actions that hurt you.
I love you. Will you forgive me?

From: _____

❀

Making Choices

Goal

To understand that the sacrament of reconciliation helps us reflect on the choices we make. Sometimes our choices are good choices, and sometimes they are not so good. Choices that turn us away from God and hurt others are called "sins."

Church Teaching

Catechism of the Catholic Church, paragraphs 1470, 1755, 1786–1789

What You Will Learn

Examples of how choices are made
The effect(s) of your good and bad choices

Supplies for this Center

Bible
6 Making Choices cards in an envelope

Directions for the Activity

- Read Matthew 25:31–45. How do the choices we make affect other people? How do they affect us?

- One by one, ask your child to read the Making Choices cards and discuss them together.

Making Choices

Your teacher has just handed out a difficult math test. Maybe you think you can't pass it unless you get some help by looking at another student's paper. You make the choice to...

Your mom asked you to clean your room. You might say to yourself, "This is my room. I'll clean it when I feel like it. I don't always have to do what my mom tells me." You make the choice to...

You're at the grocery store. You see some candy bars in a big container. You think it might be all right to take some. No one is looking. You make the choice to...

A new child at school acts a little strangely. All your friends laugh at him. They are staring at you because you are not laughing. You make the choice to...

You stayed up late Saturday night to watch TV. On Sunday morning you are too tired to get out of bed, so you think about pretending that you are sick. You make the choice to...

Your best friend just told you some gossip about another friend. You know that if you spread this gossip, you'll be the center of attention. You make the choice to...

Conversion and Reconciliation

Goal

To recall that Jesus tells a story of conversion and repentance in the parable of the prodigal son. Those who show forgiveness are like our forgiving God.

Church Teaching

Catechism of the Catholic Church, paragraphs 1439, 1465

What You Will Learn

Ways that God loves us all the time

The priest offers us the sign of God's merciful love in the sacrament of reconciliation

Supplies for this Center

Any small rings (plastic, etc.); can be purchased from a supply outlet

Bible

Four to five laminated copies of The Boy Who Ran Away, based on Luke 15:11–32

Directions for the Activity

- Decide who will take the following parts: Narrator, Younger Son, Father, Servant, and Older Son. Now read the play together. Talk about how you would feel if you were the father or one of the sons.

- Take one of the rings and place it on your child's finger as a sign of your love. (The children can keep the rings.)

The Boy Who Ran Away

(Based on Luke 15:11–32)

Narrator A father had two sons. One night the younger son said to his father…

Younger son "Dad, give me my share of the property. I want it now!"

Narrator So, his father divided the property and gave the younger son the part that was his. After a few days, the son sold his part and left home with the money. He went to a place far away where he wasted his money on reckless living. He spent everything he had, then he was left without a thing. So he went to work for one of the farmers in the country. The farmer sent him out to take care of the pigs on the farm. He wished he could eat the food the pigs had because he was so hungry. At last he came to his senses and thought:

Younger son All of my father's hired workers have more than they can eat, and here I am about to starve. I will get up and go home. I will say to my father: "Dad, I have sinned against God and against you. I am no longer fit to be called your son. Treat me as one of your hired workers."

Narrator So he got up and started back home. His dad saw him coming and was so happy to see him. He ran to his son, held him close, and kissed him tenderly.

Younger son "Dad, I have sinned against God and against you. I am no longer worthy to be called a son."

Narrator But the Father called his servants and said:

Father "Hurry, hurry, my servants, and bring my son the finest robes. Put a ring on his finger and shoes on his feet. Then let's have a feast."

Narrator Now the older son was working out in the fields. On his way back, as he drew near the house, he could hear music and dancing. Calling one of the servants, he asked, "What is going on?"

Servant "Your brother has come back. Your father has killed a fatted calf to have a feast because he is so happy to have your brother back."

Narrator But when the older son got home, he refused to join in the feast. His dad went out and pleaded with him, begging him to come in. The older son said to his dad:

Older Son "Look, all these years I have slaved for you. Never once have I disobeyed your orders. Yet you never offered me so much as a kid goat for me to celebrate with my friends. But for this son, who wasted all your property, you kill the fatted calf."

Father "My son, you are always with me, and all that I have is yours. But your brother was dead and now is alive! He was lost, but now is found."

Narrator O God, you are such a good Father to us. You love us tenderly. You know that we sin, yet you always forgive us when we return to you. We just have to rejoice. We have to be happy when we find your peace.

Being Sorry

Goal
To learn that contrition, being sorry, is a gift from God, prompted by the Holy Spirit in our hearts. It means to be sorry but also to try extra hard not to sin again.

Church Teaching
Catechism of the Catholic Church, paragraph 1451

What You Will Learn
To recite the Act of Contrition
To explain the meaning of contrition

Supplies for this Center
Bible
Three envelopes with cut-up phrases from the Act of Contrition
Pre-punched cards containing the Act of Contrition and pieces of yarn

Directions for the Activity
• Pray together Psalm 51:3–6, expressing sorrow and asking forgiveness for our sins.
• Take the words from the Act of Contrition out of the basket and as a family put them in the correct order.
• Together recite the Act of Contrition, then put the yarn through the hole to make a bookmark. The child should take the bookmark home and work on memorizing this prayer.

Activity 1

O, My God,

who are all good

and deserving of

all my love

I am sorry

for all my sins because

they displease you.

With your help

I will sin no more.

Amen.

Activity 2

○

Act of Contrition

O my God,
I am sorry
for my sins.

In choosing to do wrong
and failing to do good,
I have sinned
against you
whom I should love
above all things.

I firmly promise,
with your help,
to do penance,
to sin no more,
and to avoid
whatever leads me to sin.

Amen.

The Ten Commandments

Goal

To recall that the Ten Commandments given to Moses provide us with a way of life for keeping God's commands.

Church Teaching

Catechism of the Catholic Church, paragraphs 1822-1823

What You Will Learn

What the Ten Commandments mean for us today

The good things the Ten Commandments help us do

Supplies for this Center

One piece of colored construction paper for petals; smaller pieces of green for leaves, brown for stems, and yellow for a center circle, for each family

One piece of white paper for each family

Pencils, scissors, glue

Copies of The Ten Commandments sheet, one for each family

Laminated sample of flower model (this sample should remain on the table)

Directions for the Activity

- Read Exodus 20:1–17 and/or Deuteronomy 4:6–22. Can you name the commandments you heard in the readings? What do they mean to you?

- Take a piece of construction paper and cut ten pieces the size of flower petals. Cut the commandments from one of the copies. On each petal paste one of the commandments.

- Make the petals into a flower (as shown on the sample) by pasting them onto the white paper. Make two leaves, a stem, and a center circle (also as shown on the sample).

- On the leaves, stem, and center, write some of the good things the commandments help you to do.

- Take your flower and the Ten Commandments sheet home and discuss the Ten Commandments with your family during the week.

The Ten Commandments (and the good things they help us do)

I.   I am the Lord your God, you shall not have any strange gods before me.

II. You shall not take the name of the Lord, your God in vain.

III. Remember to keep holy the Lord's Day.

IV. Honor your father and your mother.

V.   You shall not kill.

VI. You shall not commit adultery.

VII. You shall not steal.

VIII. You shall not bear false witness against your neighbor.

IX. You shall not covet your neighbor's wife.

X.   You shall not covet your neighbor's goods.

How Many Times Must I Forgive?

Goal

To remember that God forgives us many times through our participation in the sacrament of reconciliation. Jesus asks us to forgive one another over and over.

Church Teaching

Catechism of the Catholic Church, paragraphs 277, 982

What You Will Learn

To admit that we need to forgive others

To know that God forgives us many times in the sacrament of reconciliation

Supplies for this Center

Bible

Cut out fish and place a magnet on the back of each fish

Two fish poles with string and magnet

Small container to act as a "fishpond"

Directions for the Activity

• Read Matthew 18:21–22 and discuss these questions:

  What did this mean for Peter?

  What did this mean for Jesus?

  What does this mean for you?

• Go fishing as Peter did. Take the fish pole and see what you catch.

• Answer the question on the fish that you catch. (This will help you think about forgiveness.)

You hurry home from school because you have made plans to go to a friend's house. Just as you are about to leave, you are asked to clean up your room before supper. What would you do?

You and your friend get into an argument about who is the best soccer player in the school. Your friend calls you a liar. What would you do?

It is Sunday and you do not want to go to church. What do you think you should do?

You hear in church about a famine. Many people have died and food is urgently needed. People from your church are collecting money to help. What would you do?

You are watching TV. Your older brother takes the remote and changes the station. What would you do?

Your school decides to organize a "no garbage" lunch week. The only thing you like to eat comes packaged in stuff that is not good for the environment. What would you do?

You are having trouble with some homework and everyone in the house seems too busy to help. Just then, your favorite uncle walks in and asks how you're doing. What would you do?

Your mother asks you to do your homework right after school and then she leaves for the store. Your friend comes to the door and wants to play. What will you do?

You have received some very good news and are feeling very excited. Just at that moment your friend calls and is very upset. What would you do?

Your teacher asks you to work in a group with some kids you don't like very much. What would you do?

Some kids at school are making fun of another kid because she is "different." What would you do?

You get blamed by the teacher for something you did not do. You know your friends did it. What will you do?

You are playing and someone pushes you on purpose and you get a little hurt. What can you do?

The Holy Spirit Guides Me

Goal

To recall that the Spirit of God is with us in our hearts and minds and helps us celebrate the sacrament of reconciliation.

Church Teaching

Catechism of the Catholic Church, paragraphs 976, 2736

What You Will Learn

To explain how the Spirit works in our lives and why this is important

To pray to the Spirit of God for guidance

To compose a prayer to the Holy Spirit

Supplies for this Center

Bible

Copies of the Prayers to the Holy Spirit sheet, one for each family

Four or five pencils

Directions for the Activity

- Read John 15:26, Matthew 28:19–20, or Acts 2:1–4 about the coming of the Holy Spirit. Jesus promised he would not leave us alone but would send his Spirit to be with us in our hearts.

- Unscramble the letters on the flames. What do they spell? The flames of fire are a sign of the power of the Holy Spirit in our lives.

- Make up a prayer to the Holy Spirit in the space provided.

- Together, pray the prayer you wrote. Then say the prayer "Come, Holy Spirit."

Prayers to the Holy Spirit

Unscramble the letters in the flames to complete the words below. Then, use these same words to begin a prayer to the Holy Spirit. Ask the Spirit to fill you with his gifts on the day of your First Reconciliation.

C ___ ___ ___

H ___ ___ ___

S ___ ___ ___ ___ ___

Come Holy Spirit, _____

_____

_____

Come, Holy Spirit, fill the hearts of your faithful,
and light in them the fire of your love.
Send forth your Spirit, and they shall be created,
and you shall renew the face of the earth.
Lord, by the light of your Holy Spirit,
you have taught the hearts of your faithful.
In the same Spirit help us love what is right
and always rejoice in your consolation.
We ask this through Christ our Lord. Amen.

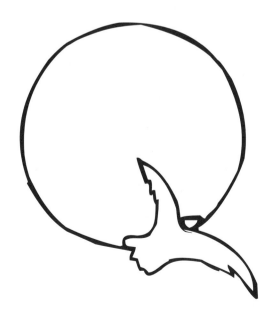

Examine Your Conscience

Goal

To learn that when we examine our conscience, we reflect on the actions of our lives, what we do or fail to do.

Church Teaching

Catechism of the Catholic Church, paragraphs 1454, 1456, 1785

What You Will Learn

To reflect on the things we do that are sins

To consider the good things we have done, as well as what things keep us from doing good

To explain the meaning of conscience

Supplies for this Center

Bible

Thinking about My Actions sheet, one for each family, to be used for an examination of conscience

Directions for the Activity

• Read Luke 6:35–38 and Psalm 119:1–5. Give examples of how God loves you and how you show love for others.

• Discuss the meaning of the word "conscience" (our inner voice). We listen to the voice inside us that tells us the difference between right and wrong.

• Quietly use the Thinking about My Actions sheet with your child. Invite your child to listen to his or her inner voice.

• Take the sheet home with you, and examine your conscience often as a family.

Thinking about My Actions

1. What happened today that makes me feel good and happy? What happened today that I feel sad about? What did I do to make someone else happy today?

2. When do I pray and talk to God? What do I put first in my life (sports, shopping, family, toys, TV)? What place does God have in my life and the life of my family?

3. Do I have reverence for God's name? Do I ever use words that are rude or crude? Do I use the name of God to express anger or disappointment, even in joking?

4. Do I participate in the liturgy on Sunday? Do I have reverence for the persons, places, and things in church? How important is my parish to me? Do I share my time, talent, and treasure with others?

5. How do I honor my parents? Do I show respect for my teachers, coaches, catechists, grandparents, and others who guide and care for me? Do I ever cause my parents to get angry or impatient with me?

6. How do I care for my pets? Do I show love and care for those in my family who are younger than me? Do I thank God for the gift of life? Do I care for creation? Do I fight on the playground or act as a bully at school or at home?

7. Do I have a space around me that is just my space, for example, my bedroom? Do I take care of it? Do I take care of my body as a holy gift from God? Do I respect other people's private space?

8. Do I respect what belongs to others? Do I take things that belong to others? Do I ever take things from stores? Do I take good care of my own things? How do I care for the environment?

9. Do I tell the truth no matter what? Do I think that "little" lies are all right? Do I say bad things about others that may not be true? Do I harm the good name of others?

10. Am I jealous of others or what they may have? Do I always want more than I have or am I satisfied with what I have? How do I care for my needy sisters and brothers?

Steps for the Sacrament of Reconciliation

Goal

To learn that the sacraments are celebrations that involve "ritual," certain words and actions that point to God's work in our lives. The sacrament of reconciliation has five ritual steps.

Church Teaching

Catechism of the Catholic Church, paragraphs 1450–1458

What You Will Learn

To review the five steps for receiving reconciliation
To explain why the sacrament is a "gift" and not just a requirement
To define the meaning of sacrament and ritual

Supplies for this Center

Bible
Pencils
Copies of A "Handy" Way to Remember, one for each person
Copies of the sheets The Rite of Penance

Directions for the Activity

- Read Matthew 16:19. Talk about the sacraments as visible signs of God's love. When we do something over and over in a certain way, it can be called a ritual. The sacrament of reconciliation is a ritual we celebrate in a certain way.

- Parents, use the expanded descriptions on the sheets The Rite of Penance to discuss the five steps with your child.

- Thank God for the gifts of love and forgiveness, and then examine your conscience.

- Pray an Act of Contrition, expressing sorrow for what you have done.

- Promise to try to do better in the future.

- Confess your sins to God in the presence of the priest.

- Do the penance the priest gives you.

A "Handy" Way to Remember

Trace your hand below. Write "Sacrament of Reconciliation" on the palm of the hand, then on each finger write one of these five rituals that help us celebrate the sacrament of reconciliation:

Examine your conscience

Be sorry for sins

Plan to do better

Confess your sins

Do penance

The Rite of Penance

1. The priest welcomes you. You greet the priest and then you make the sign of the cross together.

2. You read the word of God together. God's word gives us messages about God's love and forgiveness.

3. You confess your sins. You now open your heart to God as you tell your sins to the priest. He will never tell anyone what you have said to him. If you forget your sins, the priest will help you.

4. The priest encourages you to be a better person. He will talk to you about ways to make up for your sins. This is called a "penance."

5. The priest gives you absolution, the sign of God's forgiveness. You say a prayer of sorrow (Act of Contrition). Then you listen as the priest says the words of absolution. These words mean that God forgives you. Also, the unity with your sisters and brothers in the Church is strengthened or restored. During this time you can make the Sign of the Cross as well. At the end, answer, "Amen."

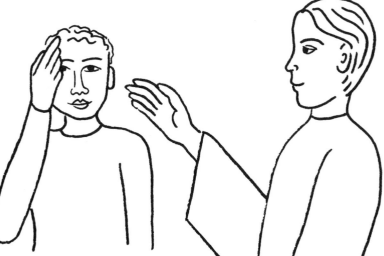

6. You and the priest give thanks to God. Together you say a prayer of thanksgiving. The priest gives you a sign of peace. You say "thank you" and then leave.

*Remember to do or say the penance the priest gives you!

Preparing for the Sacrament

Goal

To learn that all Catholics are invited to celebrate the sacrament of reconciliation.

Church Teaching

Catechism of the Catholic Church, paragraph 980

What You Will Learn

To develop a positive attitude toward the sacrament of reconciliation

To observe the ritual for first reconciliation as shown on the video

To understand the words penance and absolution

Supplies for this Center

DVD or video, TV, VCR/DVD player

Reconciliation Questions sheet for each family

Directions for the Activity

- Watch a video (or DVD) about First Reconciliation, for example, *Preparing Your Child for First Penance* (Liguori Publications) or *The Angel's First Reconciliation Lesson* (Twenty-Third Publications) or any other video of your choice.

- After viewing the video, use the Reconciliation Questions in a large or small group.

Reconciliation Questions

1. **Q** When and how does God love me?

    A *God loves me all the time, just the way I am.*

2. **Q** How do I show that I love God?

    A *I pray. I ask forgiveness. I take part in worship. I show love for others.*

3. **Q** How do I show God that I love myself?

    A *I care for myself. I learn about God and about our world. I play and I work.*

4. **Q** How do I show God that I love others?

    A *I pray for others. I help others.*

5. **Q** How do I sin?

    A *I sin by being selfish and thinking of myself first. I sin by choosing to do things that turn me away from God's love.*

6. **Q** How does God want me to forgive others?

    A *God wants me to forgive others as God forgives me. The Our Father tells me this.*

7. **Q** How and when does God forgive my sins?

    A *God forgives me totally when I am sorry for my sins. At prayer and at Mass and during the sacrament of reconciliation I ask God to forgive me.*

8. **Q** What is the sacrament of reconciliation?

    A *Reconciliation means "making up," and this sacrament is the way the Church offers us the forgiveness of Jesus.*

9. **Q** How do I celebrate this sacrament?

    A *I pray. I confess my sins. I tell God I am sorry. The priest offers me the forgiveness of Jesus.*

10. **Q** What is absolution?

    A *Absolution means that my sins are forgiven during the sacrament of reconciliation. The priest makes the sign of the cross over me and tells me in Jesus' name that I am "absolved" of my sins. I answer, "Amen."*

Learning Centers
for First Eucharist

God Loves Us

Goal

To remember that God loves each of us in a special way.

Church Teaching

Catechism of the Catholic Church, paragraphs 478, 1823

What You Will Learn

God loves each of us and helps us

We can discover new things about one another when we take the time

How our gifts and those of others can build up the kingdom of God

Supplies for this Center

Bible

Four laminated game sheets: Getting to Know One Another

Directions for the Activity

- Read Luke 19:1–10.

- Play Getting to Know One Another. Family members separate into pairs. One says a combination of a letter and a number (for example, B2); the other responds to the question in this location. Then they take turns asking and answering until they have completed all of the questions. Please leave the game sheets at the table when you are finished.

Getting to Know One Another

A	B	C
1. Who is the oldest person in your family?	1. What is your favorite outdoor game?	1. Name a time when you were scared. What did you do?
2. What is the farthest place you have ever visited?	2. What pet would you like to have?	2. What is something you really want to know about?
3. Name a time when you were very happy.	3. What is your favorite story or book?	3. What is something you worry about?
4. Who are the persons in your family?	4. What is your favorite song?	4. What is your favorite food?
5. Who is someone who helps you?	5. What is the best movie you have seen?	5. What is your favorite hobby?

The Last Supper

Goal

To recall that it was at the Passover meal that Jesus celebrated his Last Supper and to think about the ways our Mass today is like the Last Supper.

Church Teaching

Catechism of the Catholic Church, paragraph 1337

What You Will Learn

The stories of the Passover meal and the Last Supper and how to compare these to the Eucharist
What these words mean: "Do this in remembrance of me"
To recite the names of the apostles

Supplies for this Center

Bible
Pictures of the apostles and Jesus at the Last Supper: Do This in Remembrance of Me, one for each person
Four to five pencils, two to three boxes of crayons

Directions for the Activity

- Read the Bible story from Mark 14:12–25 or Luke 22:7–20. Retell the story of the Last Supper. Explain who the friends of Jesus were who shared this meal. Compare this supper to the Mass.

- Color the picture of the apostles at the Last Supper. Write the name of an apostle under each figure.

- Draw a picture of yourself at the Last Supper. Talk about how it would feel to be sitting there. How close to Jesus would you sit?

- What are some good memories you have about your Catholic faith? Why is it important to remember these things?

Do This in Remembrance of Me

Names of apostles: Peter, Andrew, John, Simon, Judas, Matthew, James, Philip, Bartholomew, Thomas, Thaddeus, James the Younger

The Mass

Goal

To learn that the Mass has a structure (ritual) of two main parts: the Liturgy of the Word and the Liturgy of the Eucharist.

Church Teaching

Catechism of the Catholic Church, paragraphs 1346–1347, 1359

What You Will Learn

The parts of the Mass in the order in which they occur (we can follow these when we worship on Sunday)

To differentiate between the two sections of the liturgy: the Liturgy of the Word and the Liturgy of the Eucharist

To understand the word Eucharist as meaning "thanksgiving"

Supplies for this Center

Bible

Four to five pencils

Drawing paper for each person

Envelopes with cutouts of the Parts of the Mass

The Order of the Mass worksheet, one for each child to take home

Directions for the Activity

• Read 1 Corinthians 11:23–26. Discuss which part of this Last Supper story sounds like words we hear at Mass.

• Take the cards naming the parts of the Mass out of the envelope and mix them up. Then, as a family, put them in the correct order. Finally, look at the sheet The Order of the Mass and see if you have them in the right order. Leave the envelopes on the table. Take your copy of The Order of the Mass to review at home.

The Order of the Mass

Introductory Rites: Coming Together

Opening Hymn and Procession: we sing and the presider comes forward to begin our time together.

Penitential Rite: we remember our sins and our need for reconciliation: "Lord, have mercy."

Gloria: we sing this joyful hymn to praise God.

Opening Prayer: the presider gathers together all our needs and presents them to God. We answer, "Amen."

Liturgy of the Word: Listening

First Reading: we listen to the lector proclaim a reading from the Old Testament. We answer, "Thanks be to God."

Psalm Response: we answer God's word to us in the first reading through the words of a psalm from the Old Testament.

Second Reading: we listen to a reading from the letters in the New Testament. We answer, "Thanks be to God."

Gospel Acclamation: we prepare to hear the good wews by standing and singing a joyful chant, usually with the word "Alleluia."

Gospel: we stand as we listen to the presider proclaim the good news about Jesus. We answer, "Praise to you, Lord Jesus Christ."

The Homily: the presider comments upon and shares insights about the readings.

The Profession of Faith: we define who we are and what we believe as a community.

General Intercessions or Prayer of the Faithful: we pray for the Church, for our world, and for one another.

Liturgy of the Eucharist: Sharing the Holy Meal

Presentation of the Gifts and Prayer over the Gifts: we bring forward what we use for the sacred meal, as well as gifts for our needy sisters and brothers.

Preface and Eucharistic Prayer: we praise and thank our creator. We remember Jesus and his last supper. We pray with the communion of saints united with the Holy Spirit, and we celebrate Jesus' continuing presence.

Communion Rite

Lord's Prayer: as we prepare to receive Communion, we pray the prayer that Jesus taught us, a petition for daily food and forgiveness.

Sign of Peace: we share a sign of peace to show we forgive and love one another.

Lamb of God: we sing this litany-song during the breaking of the bread, asking for mercy and peace.

Holy Communion: we share the body and blood of Christ.

Reflection and Prayer of Thanksgiving: we reflect and pray about what has just occurred in our lives.

Concluding Rites: The Going Forth

The Blessing and Dismissal: we are blessed and sent forth to go in peace to serve one another.

The "going forth": we say our good-byes and we often sign ourselves with holy water as we leave.

Penitential Rite

We remember our sins and our need for reconciliations: "Lord, have mercy."

Gloria

We sing this joyful hymn to praise our God.

Opening Prayer

The presider gathers together all our needs and presents them to God. We answer, "Amen."

Psalm Response

We answer God's word to us in the first reading through the words of a psalm from the Old Testament.

Gospel Acclamation

We prepare to hear the good news by standing and singing a joyful chant, usually with the word "Alleluia."

Homily

The presider shares his reflections on the message of God's word that we have just heard. We listen; sometimes we have a chance to share, too.

Presentation of the Gifts

In procession, we bring our gifts of bread and wine to the altar. These represent the gift of ourselves.

Prayer over the Gifts

The presider invites us to pray with him ("Pray, brothers and sisters…") that God will accept our gifts.

Preface

The presider begins our Eucharistic Prayer by praising God for the wonderful works of creation and redemption.

Holy, Holy, Holy Lord

At the end of the Preface, we join all creation in giving praise to the Father through Jesus.

Consecration

The words of institution and Consecration in the Eucharistic Prayer recall Jesus' actions at the Last Supper. Through these words, Jesus again becomes present in the bread and wine.

Memorial Acclamation

As we sing "Christ has died," we proclaim our belief in Jesus' death, resurrection, and final coming.

Lord's Prayer

As we prepare to receive Communion, we pray the prayer that Jesus taught us, a petition for daily food and forgiveness.

Gospel

We stand as we listen to the presider proclaim the good news about Jesus. We answer, "Praise to you, Lord Jesus Christ."

Lamb of God

We sing this litany-song during the breaking of the bread, asking for mercy and peace.

General Intercessions

We pray for those who need our care: "Lord, hear our prayer."

Prayer after Communion

The presider prays that our receiving Jesus will change us, that we may be more like Jesus.

Profession of Faith

We stand and profess what we believe in the words of the Creed: "We believe in one God...."

Blessing and Dismissal

We are sent forth to live the Eucharist with God's blessing, strength, and courage.

Second Reading

We listen to a reading from the letters in the New Testament. We answer, "Thanks be to God."

Sign of Peace

We share a sign of peace to show we forgive and love one another.

Communion

We receive Jesus in the bread and wine and say "Amen," which means "Yes, I believe."

First Reading

We listen to the lector proclaim a reading from the Old Testament. We answer, "Thanks be to God."

Opening Hymn and Procession

We begin our celebration together by praising God.

Tour of the Church

Goal

To better understand that the church is the place where we worship God, and that the people of God are also called "Church."

Church Teaching

Catechism of the Catholic Church, paragraphs 1161, 1181–1186, 1189, 1666, 2204

What You Will Learn

To identify objects in the church that are used for worship

To be comfortable and at home in the church space

To observe proper manners when you are in church

Supplies for this Center

Bible

Church Tour Items sheet, one for each participant

Tour Guide's Description Sheet, one per family

Pencils

Directions for the Activity

- Read 1 Peter 2:7–10, and discuss this as a family: What does it mean that we are the church, the people of God?

- Take a copy of the church tour checklist to church. (If possible, make the tour with someone who can show you the different items, especially if you have questions or are not familiar with the church.)

- Say the name of an object. Then find that object in the church and read the definition.

- When completed, kneel before the tabernacle where the Eucharist is reserved. As a family, say prayers of thanks for God's many gifts to you.

Tour Guide's Description Sheet

- We make the sign of the cross with water as we enter the church. We take holy water from the **font**. It is called "holy" because it has been blessed by a priest. When we sign ourselves, we recall that at baptism we were welcomed into the community of faith and share in the work of Jesus.

- In the church we can see one another, but we also focus on the **sanctuary**, the space where the altar is located. Church seats are long benches called **pews**.

- We believe that Jesus is truly present in the community that is assembled, people gathered around the **altar**. Jesus Christ is truly present in the word of God proclaimed by the reader and in the priest who presides at the worship. He is truly present in the consecrated ("made holy") bread and wine we receive at communion.

- The altar looks like a table, reminding us that Jesus comes to be our bread of life, and that we are sharing a sacred meal together. The altar is covered with an **altar cloth** (like a tablecloth) for this extraordinary meal.

- On the altar are **candles**, symbols of the presence of Jesus, the light of the world. There is also a large candle called the **Paschal** or **Easter candle**. It is a reminder of the risen Christ in our midst.

- The **lectern** is the special stand used to hold the **lectionary**, the book that contains the readings from the Bible. These are read by the lector, the reader, and by the priest, who usually stands at the lectern when he gives the homily (when he shares the meaning of the word of God with us).

- A **crucifix** is in the sanctuary. It is behind the altar and is there to remind us of the total love Jesus has for us.

- Many churches have **stained glass windows**. These show pictures from the Bible or from the lives of the saints. In the Middle Ages, when many people could not read, these were like religious picture books for them.

- Many churches have a **reconciliation room**, a place for people to come to talk with the priest, to confess their sins, and to receive the sign (absolution) that their sins are forgiven by a loving God.

- On the walls of the church there are fourteen **Stations of the Cross**. This devotion reminds us of the suffering of Jesus and the love he has for us.

- Many Catholic churches have **statues**, especially of Jesus, Mary, and the saints, perhaps St. Joseph or the patron saint of the parish. We do not worship statues, but they remind us of the great faith of Mary and the saints.

- The Blessed Sacrament chapel may be the special room where the **tabernacle** is kept. Here the consecrated hosts are reserved to bring to persons who are sick. The tabernacle also holds the ciborium with extra hosts needed for Sunday Mass. A **sanctuary light** burns to remind us that Jesus is present.

- We as the people of God are called "Church," but church is also this special place where we come together as a community of believers who praise and thank God.

Church Tour Items

Check off each item as you locate it.

- ❑ 1 Holy water font
  (Take holy water and bless yourself as you enter the church)

- ❑ 2 Baptismal font

- ❑ 3 Pews

- ❑ 4 Altar

- ❑ 6 Candles

- ❑ 7 Paschal (or Easter) candle

- ❑ 8 Lectern

- ❑ 9 Cross or crucifix

- ❑ 10 Stained glass windows

- ❑ 11 Stations of the Cross

- ❑ 12 Statues

- ❑ 13 Tabernacle

- ❑ 14 Sanctuary light

- ❑ 15 Reconciliation room

- ❑ 16 Sanctuary

- ❑ 17 Altar cloth

Objects Used for Mass

Goal

To learn about the vestments (clothing) and religious objects, signs, and symbols used to celebrate Mass.

Church Teaching

Catechism of the Catholic Church, paragraphs 1148, 1181–1186

What You Will Learn

The names of the various items used during the Mass or the celebration of the Eucharist

To recognize the vestments used at Mass

To explain how the colors of the vestments change for various seasons

Supplies for this Center

Bible

One copy of the worksheet Name These Church Objects for each family

One copy of the Can You Find It? sheet for each family to take home

Copies of the Answer Key, one for each family

Four to five pencils

Directions for the Activity

• Read Matthew 16:13–17. As a family, answer the question: "Who do you say that Jesus is?"

• Read the top half of the worksheet Name These Church Objects together. Complete it by writing the correct word under the picture. (Choose from the answers at the bottom.)

• Take the sheets home to review. You might want to take this sheet to church at some time to find the items listed there.

Name These Church Objects

As you grow in your knowledge of the Mass, you will want to learn the names and meanings of some of the objects used at Mass. Can you name any of the following? Read the descriptions on the accompanying sheet. Write the correct word below each picture, using each of the words at the bottom of the page.

1. _____

2. _____

3. _____

4. _____

5. _____

6. _____

7. _____

8. _____

9. _____

10. _____

11. _____

12. _____

13. _____

14. _____

| ciborium | sacristy | lectern | lectionary | chasuble | altar | sacramentary |
| chalice | cruets | corporal | alb | tabernacle | stole | presider's chair |

Can You Find It?

While one person reads each description below, the other can find the answer on the picture sheet. The reader should not give the answers unless the person answering is having difficulty.

1. The sacred vessels and the priest's robes are kept in this room. (*Sacristy*)

2. The priest wears this long white robe beneath his other vestments. (*Alb*)

3. The priest wears this colored robe over his long white robe. During Lent the color is purple, a symbol of penance. At Christmas and Easter the robes are white, a symbol of resurrection, birth, and rebirth. On Good Friday, Palm Sunday, Pentecost, and the feasts of martyrs, the color of the vestment is red, a symbol of the majesty of Christ and/or the action of the Holy Spirit. On Ordinary Sundays the celebrant wears green, a symbol of hope. (*Chasuble*)

4. This is worn by the priest whenever he celebrates a sacrament. It is a sign of his role as leader. (*Stole*)

5. This book contains all the prayers the priest says with us during Mass. (*Sacramentary*)

6. This cup holds the consecrated (made holy) communion hosts. (*Ciborium*)

7. This cup holds the wine that becomes the blood of Christ. (*Chalice*)

8. These hold the water and the wine used during Mass. (*Cruets*)

9. This square cloth is placed on the altar, and the priest places the ciborium and paten on it. (*Corporal*)

10. This holy book contains all the readings from the Bible used during Mass. The readings are repeated every three years. This book is carried to the altar during the opening procession. (*Lectionary*)

11. From this stand the priest, deacon, and lectors proclaim the Scripture and the priest gives the homily. (*Lectern*)

12. This is where the consecrated hosts (from the previous Mass) are kept, ready for communion for the sick or for those who wish to pray before the Blessed Sacrament. (*Tabernacle*)

12. This is where the person who presides at the Mass, the priest, sits at certain times during the Mass. (*Presider's Chair*)

14. This is where the priest prepares the sacred meal of the Eucharist. (*Altar*)

Answer Key

1. sacristy

2. alb

3. chasuble

4. stole

5. sacramentary

6. ciborum

7. chalice

8. cruets

9. corporal

10. lectionary

11. lectern

12. tabernacle

13. presider's chair

14. altar

The Apostles Creed

Goal

To recall that the Apostles Creed expresses what we believe as Catholics. The word creed means "I believe."

Church Teaching

Catechism of the Catholic Church, paragraphs 194, 2558

What You Will Learn

To list things in your life that you believe (e.g. your parents love you, the sun will rise)
To list the things you believe about your faith and your church
To learn the Apostles Creed

Supplies for this Center

Bible
A copy of the Apostles Creed scroll—What We Believe—for each family
Ribbon or yarn
Several pairs of scissors

Directions for the Activity

• Read Hebrews, chapter 11, as a review of the story of our faith in God. Have you heard of any of these people before?

• Talk to one another about some things in your life that you believe are true.

• Cut out the scroll with the words of the Apostles Creed on it. Roll it up and tie it with ribbon or yarn. While you do this, talk about what the words of the Apostles Creed mean to you.

• Take the scroll home and use it to pray and study.

What We Believe

I believe in God, the Father Almighty,
   Creator of heaven and earth;
and in Jesus Christ,
   his only Son, our Lord;
who was conceived by the Holy Spirit,
   born of the Virgin Mary,
suffered under Pontius Pilate,
   was crucified, died, and was buried.
He descended into hell;
the third day he rose again from the dead;
he ascended into heaven,
   and is seated at the right hand of God,
     the Father Almighty;
From thence he shall come to judge
   the living and the dead.
I believe in the Holy Spirit,
   the holy Catholic Church,
   the communion of saints,
   the forgiveness of sins,
   the resurrection of the body,
   and life everlasting.
Amen.

Words about the Eucharist

Goal
To learn the specific Catholic terms and words from the Bible to explain the presence of Jesus in the Eucharist.

Church Teaching
Catechism of the Catholic Church, paragraphs 1322–1323, 1329–1330

What You Will Learn
To recognize some of the words we use when we prepare to receive communion

To increase our knowledge of Scripture and the Eucharist

To develop a common language of faith

Supplies for this Center
Bible

Eight laminated Eucharist flash cards with words and Scripture references

Correct answers are on the back. Keep these cards at the learning center.

Directions for the Activity
- Use the flash cards one at a time. Find the given verses and read the quotations in the Bible.

- As a family, discuss what you think the word or phrase on the card means.

- Look on the back of the flash card to see if you have understood the meaning of the word correctly.

- Play a flash card game to see how many words and definitions each family member knows.

- Leave the flash cards at the center.

Eucharist Flash Cards
Front of Cards

Cross Matthew 16:24–25	**Breaking the Bread** Acts 2:46
Gospel Luke 4:18–19	**Memorial** Exodus 13:9
Communion 1 Corinthians 10:17	**Thanksgiving** Psalm 147:7
Lord's Supper 1 Corinthians 11:24–26	**Community** Matthew 18:20

Eucharist Flash Cards

Back of Cards

We all need to carry our own as we follow Jesus.

The disciples ate together.

Where the words and actions of Jesus are described.

You will remember that God brought our ancestors out of Egypt.

Jesus is the bread of life.

Sing praises to God with thanks.

You eat the bread and drink the wine in memory of Jesus.

When people gather together, the Lord is there with them.

The Loaves and Fishes

Goal
To understand that Eucharist is about sharing and giving to others.

Church Teaching
Catechism of the Catholic Church, paragraph 864

What You Will Learn
Retell the gospel story of the loaves and fishes
To consider ways the Eucharist invites you to share with others

Supplies for this Center
Bible
Loaves of bread (pieces will be shared with one another) and fish-shaped crackers (two for each person) in baskets
Felt board and felt figures for illustrating the story of the loaves and fishes; you can use the figures on pages 54 and 55 as samples

Directions for the Activity
- Using the felt board with figures, read (or tell) the Bible story from John 6:1–15.

- Allow children to move the felt board pieces as you tell the story.

- Pray together this meal prayer:
  Bless us, O Lord, and these your gifts,
  which we are about to receive
  from your bounty,
  through Christ our Lord. Amen.

- Break a piece of bread from the loaf in the basket and share with your family. Each family member can then take and eat two fish-shaped crackers from the basket.

Felt Board Figures

Boy   Philip or Andrew   Jesus

Basket   Five Loaves   Two Fish

Felt Board Figures

Crowd

Jesus, Our Shepherd

Goal

To recall that the Lord cares for us as a good shepherd cares for his sheep.

Church Teaching

Catechism of the Catholic Church, paragraph 1465

What You Will Learn

To reflect on the meaning of Psalm 23: "The Lord is my shepherd."

To memorize and use Psalm 23 as an after-communion prayer

Supplies for this Center

Bible

Copies of the worksheet with Psalm 23 and the sheep, one for each family

Cotton balls, four to six for each sheep

Bottles of glue

Crayons

Directions for the Activity

• Read the story of the Good Shepherd in John 10:11–18.

• Take about four to six cotton balls and pull them apart. Glue them on as wool for the sheep. Color the rest of the sheep figure.

• Together, pray Psalm 23.

Psalm 23

The Lord is my shepherd,
   I shall not want.
  He makes me lie down
   in green pastures;
he leads me beside still waters;
  he restores my soul.
He leads me in right paths
  for his name's sake.

Even though I walk
   through the darkest valley,
  I fear no evil;
for you are with me;
  your rod and your staff—
  they comfort me.

You prepare a table before me
   in the presence of my enemies;
you anoint my head with oil;
  my cup overflows.
Surely goodness and mercy shall follow
me
  all the days of my life,
and I shall dwell in the house of the Lord
  my whole life long.

Prayer

Goal

To learn that prayer to God is both formal (traditional prayer) and informal (prayer that comes from the heart).

Church Teaching

Catechism of the Catholic Church, paragraphs 2562, 2563, 2574

What You Will Learn

To recognize and recite three major prayers from our Catholic tradition: the Sign of the Cross, the Hail Mary, and the Our Father

To continue to develop an understanding of the above prayers and their importance in our lives

To compose a prayer yourself

Supplies for this Center

Bible

Three envelopes with copies of the parts of the individual prayers

A copy of the Our Catholic Prayers sheet for each family to take home to review and memorize

Copies of the Praying Hands worksheet, one for each person

Several pencils

Directions for the Activity

- Prayerfully read 1 Timothy 2:1–8.

- Open the envelopes one at a time and put the words to each prayer in order.

- Say each prayer aloud and then go on to the next envelope and prayer, always returning the phrases to their correct envelope.

- On the Praying Hands worksheet, write a prayer from your heart, thanking God for all the gifts in your life. Take the sheet home with you.

Our Catholic Prayers

Sign of the Cross

In the name of the Father,
and of the Son,
and of the Holy Spirit. Amen.

Hail Mary

Hail Mary, full of grace.
the Lord is with thee.
Blessed art thou among women,
and blessed is the fruit
of thy womb, Jesus.
Holy Mary, Mother of God,
pray for us sinners,
now and at the hour of our death. Amen.

Our Father

Our Father,
who art in heaven,
hallowed be thy name;
thy kingdom come;
thy will be done
on earth as it is in heaven.
Give us this day
our daily bread;
and forgive us our trespasses
as we forgive those
who trespass against us;
And lead us not into temptation,
but deliver us from evil. Amen.

In the name of the Father,	and of the Son.	and of the Holy Spirit. Amen.	Our Father,	who art in heaven.	hallowed be thy name;	thy kingdom come;	thy will be done
on earth as it is in heaven.	Give us this day	our daily bread;	and forgive us our trespasses	as we forgive those	who trespass against us;	And lead us not into temptation,	but deliver us from evil. Amen.
Hail Mary, full of grace,	the Lord is with thee.	Blessed art thou among women.	and blessed is the fruit	of thy womb, Jesus.	Holy Mary, Mother of God,	pray for us sinners,	now and at the hour of our death. Amen.

Praying Hands

Write your own prayer to Jesus on the lines below.

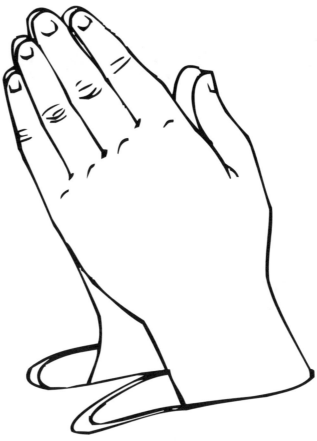

Dear Jesus,

_____

_____

_____

_____

_____

_____

_____

We Are Many Parts

Goal
To learn that, united with Jesus, we offer ourselves as a gift to God at Mass.

Church Teaching
Catechism of the Catholic Church, paragraphs 1350, 1360, 1361

What You Will Learn
To recognize that the best gift we bring to Mass is ourselves
To explain that the word Eucharist means "thanksgiving"
To name the many gifts we have to share with others

Supplies for this Center
Bible
Copies of My Gifts worksheet, one for each person
Several black markers
Crayons

Directions for the Activity
- Read 1 Corinthians, chapters 12–13, and list the gifts Paul mentions. What are some gifts that each of you has?
- Color the picture. On each grape, write one gift you or your family has to share with the rest of the church community.
- Write your name on the chalice to remind yourself that you, too, are part of the Body of Christ.
- After completing the worksheet, talk with one another about the various gifts members of your family have.

My Gifts
What gifts has God given me to share?

On each grape, write a gift you can share with others. Then write your name on the chalice.

I Am the Vine

Goal

To recall that we are all part of the church community and our strength (grace) comes through Jesus.

Church Teaching

Catechism of the Catholic Church, paragraphs 787, 789, 1213, 1988, 2074

What You Will Learn

To recognize other people who are part of our church community

To explain how Jesus is like the vine and we are like the branches

Supplies for this Center

Bible

Copies of worksheet I Am the Vine, one per person

Several black markers

Crayons

Directions for the Activity

- Read John 15:1–8 from the Bible. This passage talks about the vine and branches. What do these words mean to you?

- Take one of the I Am the Vine worksheets, and on each of the leaves write the name of someone you know who belongs to your parish church.

- Color the vine (tree) and the branches (leaves).

- Talk about the names you wrote on your leaves. Why did you choose those persons?

I Am the Vine

Jesus said:
"I am the vine,
you are the branches."

Baptism

Goal
To learn that baptism begins our entrance into the Christian community and is the first sacrament of initiation we receive. (Eucharist is the second.) During baptism, we renew our vows and promise to be faithful to God.

Church Teaching
Catechism of the Catholic Church, paragraphs 1265, 1267

What You Will Learn
To listen to stories about your baptism day
To experience water as a sign of your baptism
To renew your baptismal vows
To give thanks for the gift of baptism

Supplies for this Center
Bible
Copy of worksheet My Baptism for each person
Holy water font or bowl
Several pencils

Directions for the Activity
- Read Romans 6:1–4. What does this passage tell you about baptism, the first sacrament you received?

- Take a copy of the My Baptism worksheet, discuss it, then complete the questions about your baptism. (Children will need some help with this.)

- Go into the church, if possible, near the baptismal font. (If you cannot go to the church, have a dish of water at the center.)

- An adult reads the statements of faith from Baptismal Promises, and all respond: "I do" after each statement.

- All bless one another on the forehead with holy water.

- Together, slowly make the sign of the cross.

My Baptism

What is the date of your baptism? _____

Why did your parents choose the name they gave you? _____

Who are your godparents? _____

Who came to witness and celebrate your baptism? _____

In which parish were you baptized? _____

Do you know what the baptismal water means that is poured on your head or body?

_____

Have you ever seen someone baptized? What do you remember? _____

_____

Baptismal Promises

(A parent reads the questions below and the whole family answers.)

Do you reject Satan? (I do!)

And all his works? (I do!)

And all his empty promises? (I do!)

Do you reject the glamour of evil and refuse to be controlled by sin? (I do!)

Do you believe in God, the Father Almighty, creator of heaven and earth? (I do!)

Do you believe in Jesus Christ, his only Son, our Lord, who was born of the Virgin Mary, was crucified, died, and was buried, rose from the dead, and is now seated at the right hand of the Father? (I do!)

Do you believe in the Holy Spirit, the holy Catholic Church, the communion of saints, the forgiveness of sins, the resurrection of the body, and life everlasting? (I do!)

This is our faith, the faith of our church. We are proud to believe in Christ Jesus our Lord. (Amen!)

The Church

Goal

To reinforce that the church is a building, but more importantly, that we the people of God are the Church.

Church Teaching

Catechism of the Catholic Church, paragraphs 1140, 1181, 1186

What You Will Learn

To explain the different meanings of the word "church"

To reflect on the words: "The church makes the Eucharist and the Eucharist makes the Church."

Supplies for this Center

Bible

Several pairs of scissors

Crayons

Pattern for a church building, We Are the Church, one for each family

Smiley face stickers or people stickers

Directions for the Activity

• How is the church described in Matthew 18:20 or 1 Corinthians 12:12–28?

• Each family takes one of the We Are the Church sheets and cuts out the model of a church.

• Color and decorate. Add people to your church, using stickers or drawing figures.

We Are the Church

Color, decorate, and add people to your church.

Front

Back of Church

Front

THE CHURCH

WE ARE

Inside

Front

WE ARE

THE CHURCH

Preparing for First Eucharist

Goal
To reinforce that Catholics rejoice in sharing the Body and Blood of Jesus as often as possible.

Church Teaching
Catechism of the Catholic Church, paragraphs 1324, 1333

What You Will Learn
To develop a greater love for the Eucharist

To receive the Eucharist correctly

To practice saying "Amen" (saying "yes" to what we receive and to what we are)

Supplies for this Center
Bible

Receiving First Communion worksheet, one for each person

Small cards with word "Amen" on them

Crayons

Directions for the Activity
- Read 1 Corinthians 17:27–29.

- Watch a video, for example, *Preparing Your Child for First Communion* (Liguori Publications), or *The Angel's First Reconciliation Lesson* (Twenty-Third Publications).

- Discuss the procedure for receiving First Communion using the Receiving First Communion worksheet. Discuss receiving both the bread and the wine.

- Practice saying "Amen," as you will when you are given the bread and cup.

- Review how to hold your hands for receiving communion and how to take the cup from the minister. Take the sheets home with you.

Receiving First Communion

Here are some ways we can show reverence and respect for the Eucharist.

- Walk slowly toward the eucharistic minister, reflecting that you are giving yourself to Jesus as you receive the bread of life.
- Bow reverently before receiving communion.
- Receive both bread and wine (the Body and Blood of Jesus) when both are offered.
- Receive the bread by making a table with your hands.
- Say "Amen" loudly and clearly and look at the priest or eucharistic minister.
- Fold your hands and prayerfully return to your seat.
- Sing the communion hymn.

Here are some ways we can show reverence and respect for other persons who are the body of Christ.

- Wait reverently for your turn. Be aware of others around you.
- Give others the sign of peace and thoughtfully pray the Our Father.
- Pray for others who are receiving the eucharistic meal together with you at the table of the Lord.
- Sing the communion song with the community.
- Keep a reverent silence (except for the song) after you have received the Body and Blood of Christ.

Learning Centers for the Whole Community

No matter what form your parish whole community catechesis takes, learning centers can be an effective part of the process. They allow children and their families to individualize their learning, to pace it according to their needs. The learning centers recommended in this section of the book are elements of four sessions that focus on First Reconciliation and four that focus on First Eucharist. These sessions can be part of monthly gatherings or aspects of weekly faith formation sessions with children. They involve families in the preparation process and encourage adults as well as children to learn about and share their faith.

Note that these sessions require a facilitator, someone who will set up the learning centers, lead the prayers and discussions, and generally guide the process of moving through the materials.

Celebrating Forgiveness

Goal

To recall that the sacrament of reconciliation calls us to make peace with God and one another.

Notes to Facilitator

Before participants arrive, set up a prayer area with the Bible enthroned. When all have arrived, light a candle and invite one of the adult participants to proclaim the word of God from Luke 15:11–32; use the play "The Boy Who Ran Away" from page 13, if you wish. If you use the play, assign parts and allow time for practice before "proclaiming" it.

At the conclusion of the reading or the play, invite an adult to present each child with a ring as a symbol of forgiveness. He or she might say, for example, "Let this ring remind you of God's never-ending love and forgiveness."

Now divide participants into groups of six to eight. Be sure there are children in every group. Invite each group to complete these two learning centers: Making Peace with God and Others (page 8) and Steps for the Sacrament of Reconciliation (page 24).

When the groups have completed the activities, allow time for sharing what they experienced. Then invite them to discuss these questions:

- In the Prodigal Son story, which character are you most like, or with whom do you most identify and why?

- How can you reconcile with someone you have offended, or reconcile with someone who has offended you?

- How does it feel to be reconciled with God in the sacrament of reconciliation?

After this discussion, gather around the prayer space and together recite the Prayer of St. Francis.

Prayer of St. Francis

Take this prayer home and pray it often.

Make me, O Lord, an instrument of your peace.
Where there is hatred, let me sow love;
Where there is injury, pardon;
Where there is doubt, faith;
Where there is despair, hope;
Where there is darkness, light;
Where there is sadness, joy.

O Divine Master,
grant that I may not so much
seek to be consoled as to console;
to be understood as to understand;
to be loved as to love.
For it is in giving that we receive;
it is in pardoning that we are pardoned,
and it is in dying
that we are born to eternal life.
Amen.

Examination of Conscience

Goal

To recognize our conscience as the "small inner voice" that develops over time and helps us distinguish right from wrong.

Notes to Facilitator

Before participants arrive, set up a prayer space with the Bible enthroned. When all have arrived, light a candle and invite one of the adult participants to proclaim the word of God from Matthew 25:31–46.

At the conclusion of the reading, invite participants to discuss the following questions:

- What keeps us from doing the good we know we should do?
- What do we mean by the word conscience?
- How do the choices we make affect other people?

Now divide the participants into groups of six to eight. Be sure there are children in every group. Invite each group to complete these three learning centers: Examine Your Conscience (page 22), Making Choices (page 10), The Ten Commandments (page 16).

When the groups have completed the activities, allow time for sharing what they experienced. With the help of the group, challenge the children to recall the Ten Commandments from memory.

After this activity, invite all to gather around the prayer space as you lead the Ten Commandments Prayer Service.

Ten Commandments Prayer Service

Leader   May we always turn to our God rather than to things or power to take God's place.

All   *Lord, help us hear your voice.*

Leader   May we not take God's name in vain or use God's name in a disrespectful way.

All   *Lord, help us hear your voice.*

Leader   May we keep Sunday holy by seriously looking for God-time and family time in our lives.

All   *Lord, help us hear your voice.*

Leader   May we honor those who have helped and are now helping us be the good people we are today.

All   *Lord, help us hear your voice.*

Leader   May we protect, honor, and care for all of life.

All   *Lord, help us hear your voice.*

Leader   May we love truly, love rightly, love even when it hurts, and love so it lasts.

All   *Lord, help us hear your voice.*

Leader   May we never be afraid to speak the truth, even when it costs us.

All   *Lord, help us hear your voice.*

Leader   May we believe that stealing is about more than just getting caught.

All   *Lord, help us hear your voice.*

Leader   May we be satisfied with what we have and not always want more.

All   *Lord, help us hear your voice.*

Leader   Loving God, you guide us on our way. Help us listen to your words and your laws and always come to you for help when we are in need. We ask this in the name of Jesus.

All   *Amen.*

A Sign of God's Mercy

Goal

To accept the sacrament of reconciliation as a sign of God's loving forgiveness and mercy in our lives.

Notes to Facilitator

Before participants arrive, set up a prayer space with the Bible enthroned. When all have arrived, light a candle and invite one of the adult participants to proclaim the word of God from Acts 2:2–4. Then all bow their heads and together pray the "Act of Contrition" (see the bookmark on page 15).

Now divide participants into groups of six to eight. Be sure there are children in every group. Invite each group to complete these two learning centers: The Holy Spirit Guides Me (page 20), and Being Sorry (page 14).

When the groups have completed the activities, allow time for sharing what they experienced. Then invite them to discuss the following questions:

- As the Holy Spirit guides you, how do your parents and other adults guide you?

- How can the Holy Spirit (whom you cannot see) help you prepare for the sacrament of reconciliation?

- What is contrition? What does it mean to be contrite? Can you think of some examples?

When the discussion is completed, gather together at the prayer space. Give all a moment for recollection, then ask group members to make up and share their own prayers of sorrow or contrition. When everyone has had a chance to pray, share with one another some sign of peace before departing.

Forgiving Others

Goal

To recall that we are to forgive others as we are forgiven: "Forgive us our trespasses."

Notes to Facilitator

Before participants arrive, set up a prayer space with the Bible enthroned. When all have arrived, light a candle and invite one of the adult participants to proclaim the word of God from Matthew 18:21–22. At the conclusion of the reading, all join hands and pray the Our Father.

Now divide the participants into groups of six to eight. Be sure there is a child in every group. Provide each group with a game board, We Are God's Work of Art! (page 5). When the groups have had sufficient time to enjoy the game, invite them to discuss these questions about the meaning of penance.

- When and where do we experience forgiveness?

- How do we "make up" when we have offended others?

- Another expression for making up may be "doing penance." Have you ever had to do a penance? Why? Do you sometimes choose to do a penance, for example, during Lent? Why?

Now ask the same groups of six to eight to complete these two learning centers: Families Forgive (page 6) and How Many Times Must I Forgive? (page 18). Depending on the size of the group, you may have to provide more than one of these centers so everyone has time to discuss the questions.

When the groups have completed the activities, allow time for sharing what they experienced. After the sharing time, gather around the prayer space. Give each person a small "fish" made of shiny paper with the word "forgive" on it. Pin this on each person's jacket as a reminder that we all need to forgive and be forgiven. Conclude by singing a reconciliation hymn together. (Look through your parish's hymnal for a list of appropriate songs.)

Prayer and Ritual

Goal

To appreciate the sacraments as signs of God's love for us. Prayer and ritual are the focus of all the sacraments.

Notes to Facilitator

Before participants arrive, set up a prayer area with the Bible enthroned. Also have a bowl of holy water and something to sprinkle it with. When all have arrived, light a candle and invite one of the adult participants to proclaim the word of God from 1 Timothy 2:1–8.

At the conclusion of the reading, lead all in a centering prayer. Ask everyone to close their eyes, place their hands on their diaphragm (demonstrate), breathe in and out and begin to repeat, first softly and then silently, "Lord Jesus Christ, have mercy on me." During this time, remind all to listen to God speak to their hearts.

When all have had sufficient time for this to be a meaningful experience, invite them to discuss the following questions:

- How do you talk to God when you pray?

- What are your favorite prayers? Are they traditional prayers or those you make up from your heart? Have you ever meditated, as we just did, as part of your prayer?

After this discussion, an adult can hold the large bowl of water and the sprinkler and ask:

- What happens at a baptism you have witnessed in church?

- Why is it a good idea to renew our baptismal vows often?

Then generously sprinkle everyone with holy water while each makes the Sign of the Cross.

Now divide participants into groups of six to eight. Be sure there are children in every group. Invite each group to complete four learning centers: Prayer (page 58), The Apostles Creed (page 48), Baptism (page 66), and Jesus, Our Shepherd (page 56).

When the groups have completed these activities, allow time for sharing what they have experienced.

After this discussion, gather around the prayer space and reverently read or say together Psalm 23 (page 57).

The Church

Goal

To learn that the church is a building, but more importantly, that we the people are the Church. The parish church is a special place where we come to worship as a community.

Notes to Facilitator

Before participants arrive, set up a prayer area with the Bible enthroned. When all have arrived, light a candle and invite one of the adult participants to proclaim the word of God from 1 Corinthians 12:12–27. Then sing together "We Are Many Parts" (from the *Gather Two Hymnal*).

At the conclusion of the reading and song, divide the participants into groups of six to eight people. Be sure there are children in every group. Invite each group to complete three learning centers: We Are Many Parts (page 62), The Church (page 68), and Objects Used for Mass (page 44).

When the groups have completed the activities, allow time for sharing what they have experienced. Then invite them to discuss these questions:

- What is the church?

- How are we connected to Jesus in the church community?

- Why are the objects and items we use in church important for our worship?

- To what other communities do you belong?

When the discussion is completed, encourage the groups to take the church tour (using pages 41–43) as they walk through the church. At the completion of the tour, invite the participants to kneel quietly in the church or in the Blessed Sacrament chapel to pray alone or together.

Breaking of the Bread

Goal

To name the connection between the Passover, the Last Supper, and the Mass.

Notes to Facilitator

Before participants arrive, set up a prayer area with the Bible enthroned and a basket with a large loaf of bread. When all have arrived, light a candle and invite one of the adult participants to proclaim the word of God from Luke 22:7–21 and Exodus 12:1–14. After the reading, pass the loaf of bread and invite all to take a piece to eat. Then say together the common meal prayer: "Bless us, O Lord, and these thy gifts, which we are about to receive from thy bounty, through Christ our Lord. Amen."

After the prayer, invite the participants to discuss the following questions:

- What does Passover mean to you?

- What took place at the Last Supper?

- What part of the Mass means the most to you?

Now divide the participants into groups of six to eight. Be sure there are children in every group. Invite each group to complete these three learning centers: Words about the Eucharist (page 50), The Loaves and Fishes (page 53), and The Last Supper (page 34).

When the groups have completed these activities, allow time for sharing what they have experienced. Then invite them to discuss these questions:

- What do celebrating the Eucharist and celebrating Thanksgiving dinner in your homes have in common? ("Eucharist" means thanksgiving.)

- How are they different?

- How do we show we are grateful?

After this discussion, gather around the prayer space and watch a video of the Last Supper if one is available to you. Then sing together a eucharistic hymn such as "Song of the Body of Christ" (David Haas), or any other appropriate song.

The Mass

Goal

To recognize the Mass as the greatest prayer. It is here we remember and receive Jesus, the Bread of Life. It is here we share our faith with the assembly, the church community.

Notes to Facilitator

Before participants arrive, set up a prayer area with the Bible enthroned. When all have arrived, light a candle and together sing a familiar "Alleluia." Then invite one of the adult participants to read the word of God from 1 Corinthians 11:23–29 or from John 15:3–5. Ask all to offer spontaneous prayers of the faithful for their/our needs. All respond, "Lord, hear our prayer." Then invite all to share a sign of peace.

Now divide the participants into groups of six to eight. Be sure there are children in every group. Invite each group to complete these three learning centers: God Loves Us (page 32), The Mass (page 36), and I Am the Vine (page 64).

When the groups have completed the activities, allow time for sharing what they have experienced. Then invite them to discuss these questions:

- Why is the Mass the greatest prayer?

- Do you ever have to make a sacrifice? What does this mean? Why did Jesus sacrifice himself for us?

- Why do you think it is important to participate in the Mass on Sunday (or Saturday evening)?

- How is Christ present in the assembly, in the word, in the presider, and especially in the Eucharist?

After the discussion, assemble as a large group to view a video about preparing for First Eucharist.

When the video is finished, gather around the prayer space and sing a familiar form of "Holy, Holy, Holy"," Christ Has Died," and "Amen."

Appendix

Letter to parents for First Reconciliation

Notes to Facilitator

Have copies of this letter available for each family to read before they begin visiting the learning centers. Feel free to personalize it by including the dates for your First Reconciliation and First Eucharist celebrations plus any other information you want them to have.

Dear Parents,

Congratulations on having your child prepare for the celebration of reconciliation. In order to help you experience this time with him or her, we ask that you please complete each of these twelve learning centers as directed. You can complete them with your child (and other family members) in any order you wish. A sheet with directions will be provided for each center. It tells you what the goals are and what you and your child will learn. It also gives directions for the activity. At each center you will find a copy of paragraphs from the *Catechism of the Catholic Church*, plus the supplies that will be provided for the activities. When you have finished a center, please take your projects with you and leave it as you found it for the next family. Doing the activities at all the learning centers should take about two to three hours. Please don't rush. Take all the time you need to share the Scripture readings and activities and to answer any questions your child might have. If there are questions you need help with, please let me know.

Here are the names and numbers of each learning center:

1. Building Self-Esteem
2. Families Forgive
3. Making Peace with God and Others
4. Making Choices
5. Conversion and Reconciliation
6. Being Sorry
7. The Ten Commandments
8. How Many Times Must I Forgive?
9. The Holy Spirit Guides Me
10. Examine Your Conscience
11. Steps for the Sacrament of Reconciliation
12. Preparing for the Sacrament

Thank you for coming to spend this time with your child. May you learn more about the sacrament of reconciliation and so more actively guide and prepare your child to celebrate it.

Letter to Parents for First Eucharist

Notes to Facilitator

Have copies of this letter available for each family to read before they begin visiting the learning centers. Feel free to personalize it by including the dates for your First Reconciliation and First Communion celebrations plus any other information you want them to have.

Dear Parents,

Congratulations! Your child is preparing for the wondrous celebration of First Eucharist! To help you experience this with him or her, we ask that you please complete each of these learning centers as directed. You can complete them with your child (and other family members) in any order you wish. A sheet with directions will be provided for each center. It tells you what the goals are and what you and your child will learn. It also gives directions for the activity. At each center you will find a copy of paragraphs from the *Catechism of the Catholic Church*, plus the supplies that will be provided for the activities. When you have finished a center, please take your projects with you and leave it as you found it for the next family. The activities for all the learning centers should take about three hours or so. Please don't rush. Take all the time you need to share the Scripture readings and activities and to answer any questions your child might have. If there are questions you need help with, please let me know.

Here are the names and numbers of each learning center.

1. God Loves Us
2. The Last Supper
3. The Mass
4. Tour of the Church
5. Objects Used for Mass
6. The Apostles Creed
7. Words about the Eucharist
8. The Loaves and Fishes
9. Jesus, Our Shepherd
10. Prayer
11. We Are Many Parts
12. I Am the Vine
13. Baptism
14. The Church
15. Preparing for First Eucharist

Thank you for coming to spend this time with your child. May you learn more about the Eucharist and so more actively guide and prepare your child to celebrate the sacrament.

Evaluation Form

Parents, when you've completed the learning centers,
please complete this evaluation. Thank you.

The number of times I have participated in learning centers with this child: _____

In total I was able to spend: _____1 hour _____2 hours _____hours

Things my child and I found helpful through doing the activities, readings, and so on of the centers include (check all that apply):

____Having a place and time to adequately focus on the themes
____Spending quality time together
____Having the opportunity to talk about faith
____Having the supportive presence of other parents and children
____Other (Please specify):_____

Things my child and I found difficult with the centers (check all that apply):

____Scheduled days   ____Activities (explain): _____
____Time of day   ____Other (please specify): _____

Centers could be improved by:

Do you have any other comments about the use and value of the learning centers?

_____   _____
Your name   Date

Group Gathering Prayers for First Reconciliation

All participants should gather in an area that is prepared with the enthroned Bible, a candle, a banner, and a cross.

Leader	We gather together in the name of the Father, and of the Son, and of the Holy Spirit.
All	Amen.
Opening Song	"Standin' in the Need of Prayer" or other appropriate song
Leader	Father, God, you are loving and forgiving. We come to you with hearts full of love, though we know that we have sinned. Help us be more faithful and follow your Son Jesus so we can grow in love of you and one another. We ask this in Jesus' name. Amen.
Gospel	John 10:11–17
Action	Give each child a sheep pattern (page 57). Have each put his or her name on it and pin it to the large banner. This banner may then be placed in an area where the entire parish community can see it and remember to pray for these children as they prepare for the celebration of the sacrament of reconciliation.
Prayer together	Act of Contrition (page 15)
Closing Song	"Peace Is Flowing Like a River" or other appropriate song

Children and parents can now begin to work at the various learning centers.

First Reconciliation Prayers
for Individual Families

All gather in a quiet area that is prepared with the enthroned Bible (open to Luke 15:1–7), a candle, a banner, and a cross, with soft music in the background. Provide three or four chairs.

Families and children sit quietly for a few moments listening to the music. Then make the Sign of the Cross together: "In the name of the Father, and of the Son, and of the Holy Spirit. Amen."

Prayer	Father, God, you are loving and forgiving. We come to you with hearts full of love, though we know that we have sinned. Help us be more faithful and follow your Son Jesus so we can grow in love of you and one another. We ask this in Jesus' name.
Child	Amen.
Gospel	Luke 15:1–7
Action	The child can now take a sheep pattern (page 57), put his or her name on it, and pin it to the large banner. This banner may then be placed in an area where the entire parish community can see it and remember to pray for these children as they prepare for the celebration of the sacrament of reconciliation.
Parent	Lord, have mercy.
Child	Lord, have mercy.
Parent	Christ, have mercy.
Child	Christ, have mercy.
Parent	Lord, have mercy.
Child	Lord, have mercy.

Each child can now hold the cross and say the Act of Contrition (page 15).

Parent	Dear God, you want us to know more about you. Be with us as we begin these centers where we will learn more about you and about one another. We pray in Jesus' name.
Child	Amen.

Children and parents can now begin to work at the various learning centers.

Group Gathering Prayers
for First Eucharist

All participants should gather in an area that is prepared with the enthroned Bible, a candle, a banner, a cross, a dish of holy water, a loaf of bread, a cup (chalice) of grape juice (wine).

Leader   We gather together in the name of the Father, and of the Son, and of the Holy Spirit.

All   Amen.

Opening Song   "Let Us Break Bread Together," verses 1 and 2, or another appropriate song

Leader   Father, God, you gave us hearts to love you and to love one another. Fill our hearts more each day with your love. Help us be always grateful for this love. We ask this in Jesus' name. Amen.

Reading   1 Corinthians 11:23–26

Action   Each child should bring a picture of himself or herself. Pin these to the large banner. This banner may then be placed in an area where the entire parish community can see it and remember to pray for these children as they prepare for the celebration of the sacrament of the Eucharist.

All   Our Father, who art in heaven…

Closing Song   Now pass the loaf of bread around and invite each to take a piece and eat it. During this time, sing verse three of "Let Us Break Bread Together" or another appropriate song.

Children and parents can now begin to work at the various learning centers.

First Eucharist Prayers for Individual Families

Family members should gather in a quiet area that is prepared with the enthroned Bible (open to 1 Corinthians 11:23–26), a candle, a banner, a small dish of holy water, and a loaf of bread, with soft music playing in the background. Provide three or four chairs.

Family members sit quietly for a few moments listening to the music. Then each bless themselves with holy water: "In the name of the Father, and of the Son, and of the Holy Spirit. Amen."

Prayer　　Father, God, you are loving and forgiving. We come to you with hearts full of love, though we know that we have sinned. Help us be more faithful and follow your Son Jesus so we can grow in love of you and one another. We ask this in Jesus' name.

Child　　Amen.

Reading　　1 Corinthians 11:23–26

Action　　The child should take a picture of himself or herself and pin it to the large banner. (This banner may then be placed in an area where the entire parish community can see it and remember to pray for these children as they prepare for the celebration of the sacrament of the Eucharist.)

Prayer together　　Our Father, who art in heaven…

Have a dish set out with small pieces of bread on it. Each family member may now take one and eat it.

Parent　　Dear Jesus, you will soon give yourself to us as the Bread of Life. Help us be worthy of this great gift. We pray in your holy name.

Child　　Amen.

Children and parents can now begin to work at the various learning centers.